CONTENTS

Emersons Green Primary School

Coming to England
by Floella Benjamin

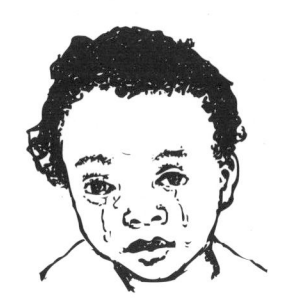

INTRODUCTION
Coming to England by Floella Benjamin — 3

WAYS IN
This is your life — 4
What is autobiography? — 5
Is it autobiography? — 6
Chapter titles — 7

MAKING SENSE
Life in Trinidad — 8
The family breaks up — 10
The journey — 11
Life in England — 13
Double identity — 14
Success — 15

DEVELOPING IDEAS
Marmie — 16
The Queen's English — 18
Ellington's fight — 20
Weather — 21
Names — 22
Land of Hope and Glory — 24

EVALUATION
Interviewing Floella Benjamin — 25
Afterword — 26

HELP!
Using this book — 27
Teachers' notes — 29

READ & RESPOND

1

CREDITS

Published by Scholastic Ltd,
Villiers House,
Clarendon Avenue,
Leamington Spa,
Warwickshire CV32 5PR
Text © 2001 Angel Scott
© 2001 Scholastic Ltd
1 2 3 4 5 6 7 8 9 0   1 2 3 4 5 6 7 8 9 0

Author Angel Scott
Editor Roanne Davis
Assistant editor Dulcie Booth
Series designer Lynne Joesbury
Designer Lynda Murray
Illustrations Jane Bottomley
Cover illustration Michael Frith

Designed using Adobe Pagemaker

British Library Cataloguing-in-Publication Data
A catalogue record for this book is available from the British Library.

ISBN 0-439-01851-X

The right of Angel Scott to be identified as the Author of this work has been asserted by her in accordance with the Copyright, Designs and Patents Act 1988.

All rights reserved. This book is sold subject to the condition that it shall not, by way of trade or otherwise, be lent, hired out or otherwise circulated without the publisher's prior consent in any form of binding or cover other than that in which it is published and without a similar condition, including this condition, being imposed upon the subsequent purchaser.

No part of this publication may be reproduced, stored in a retrieval system, or transmitted, in any form or by any means, electronic, mechanical, photocopying, recording or otherwise, without the prior permission of the publisher. This book remains copyright, although permission is granted to copy those pages marked as 'photocopiable' for classroom distribution and use only in the school which has purchased the book, or by the teacher who has purchased the book, and in accordance with the CLA licensing agreement. Photocopying permission is given for purchasers only and not for borrowers of books from any lending service.

ACKNOWLEDGEMENTS

Pavilion Books Ltd for the use of text and the front cover of *Coming to England* by Floella Benjamin, Text © 1995, Floella Benjamin; Cover illustration © 1995, Michael Frith (1995, Pavilion Books Ltd); **Peters Fraser and Dunlop Group** for the use of 'Names' by Jackie Kay from *Three Has Gone* by Jackie Kay © 1994, Jackie Kay (1994, Blackie).

INTRODUCTION

Coming to England
by Floella Benjamin

ABOUT THIS BOOK

Coming to England is the autobiography of Floella Benjamin's early years. It tells the real-life story of how she and her family left their home in Trinidad and came to live in England in 1960. The journey across 4000 miles of ocean took 15 days. In the book she describes the contrast between her home and life on a Caribbean island and the home and life she came to in London. Everything was different, but the hardest and most upsetting part of her new life was the racism she encountered. Children and adults were unkind, hostile and cruel because she was different and they felt that she did not belong in a country that she had been brought up to believe was as much hers as theirs – Trinidad was part of the British Empire.

The book describes how Floella, through the love and support of her close-knit family, and particularly her mother, learned how to survive and succeed.

ABOUT FLOELLA BENJAMIN

After leaving school, Floella Benjamin went into show business and appeared in a number of stage shows before moving on to television work. She became a presenter on BBC children's programmes *Playschool* and *Playaway*. In 1987 she and her husband set up their own television company to make programmes and videos for young people. She has also written several books for children.

Floella wrote this book, *Coming to England*, "to give young people, both black and white, an insight into the circumstances that brought a whole generation of West Indians to Britain". By describing her own experiences she hoped to bring to life what it had been like for many others; how difficult and painful it had been for them to be rejected and made to feel that they did not belong "in the fabled motherland, the 'Land of Hope and Glory'". In the closing sentence of the book she says: "I hope this book will go some way in helping people to find their identity, to discover where they came from and to feel proud of themselves."

This is your life

In an autobiography, an author writes the story of his or her own life. It is a type of non-fiction based on memories of real experiences. The writer may include facts such as dates, and names of people and places, but because autobiography is personal writing, the 'facts' may not always be 'true'. People remember things differently.

- Think about your own life story.
  What have you been told about your early life?
  Does it match your memories?
  How could you verify it?

- Make some notes about your life story.

Things I have been told (such as significant moments of your life)	My memories	Information (such as certificates and medals, photographs, souvenirs)

- Start to gather information for your autobiography while you begin reading Floella Benjamin's.

What is autobiography?

- What do you know about autobiography writing? Read this list and put
✔ if you think the statement applies to autobiography
✗ if you think it doesn't
or O if you think it sometimes does.

☐ Has one main character, who is also the author.

☐ Is written in the first person.

☐ Is about key moments in the writer's life.

☐ Is only written by famous people.

☐ Describes main influences (people, events, places) on the writer.

☐ Has a moral or message for readers.

☐ Describes people's relationships with the writer.

☐ Shows the writer's feelings, thoughts, reactions and beliefs.

☐ Is based on things that actually happened.

☐ Is all made up.

☐ Is about real people, events and places.

☐ Is factual writing about someone else's life.

☐ Contains some facts.

☐ Tells about events in the order they really happened.

☐ Is partly made up and partly factual.

☐ All happens in the past.

☐ Is written to entertain readers.

☐ Is written to inform readers of facts.

Photocopiable — Coming to England

Is it autobiography?

● Look carefully at the cover and the first pages (up to the end of page 1). Is *Coming to England* an autobiography or not? How can you tell?

Autobiography	Example from *Coming to England*
Is written by someone with an interesting true story to tell.	
Tells the writer's life story.	
The main character is the writer.	
Shows the writer's feelings, thoughts and beliefs.	
Is based on what really happened.	
Is written to entertain and inform readers.	
Sometimes has a moral or a lesson to be learned.	
I think *Coming to England* is / is not autobiography because	

Chapter titles

● Here are some chapter titles from *Coming to England*. From what you have found out about the book, can you guess what Floella Benjamin writes about in each one? (Remember the kind of writing it is!)

Chapter title	In this chapter, Floella...
Life in Trinidad	
School Life	
Celebrations	
Coming to England	
The Last Goodbye	
Life at Sea	
Land of Hope and Glory	
Settling In	
Survival	
Breaking Down the Barriers	

Life in Trinidad

In the first five chapters, Floella tells us about life in Trinidad, about herself, and about her family.

● Find information about each of these topics by skimming through the chapters to find the relevant pages. Then scan those pages to find key points. Make some notes for each topic.

The country of Trinidad

Floella and her family

Coming to England

Photocopiable

Life in Trinidad (cont.)

Making sense

The family house and garden

Food and shopping

Floella's life: school, church, outings, celebrations

● What things are different about Floella's life in Trinidad to your own life? What things are similar? Write your answers on the back of this sheet.

Photocopiable

READ & RESPOND

Coming to England

The family breaks up

- Read the chapter 'Coming to England.'

What were the reasons *for* moving to England?

What were Floella's reasons *against* the move?

- Find information in the book that tells you what life was like for the children before and after Marmie left for England.

Life before she left	Life after she left

Coming to England

The journey

- Read 'The Last Goodbye', 'Life at Sea', 'Land Ahoy' and 'Land of Hope and Glory'. Use the game board to turn the children's sea voyage into a snakes-and-ladders type game for four players.

Good things that happen on the journey move players forward. Bad things move them backwards.

- Make a list of main events from when the children receive the letter (page 49). Then decide whether each event is a good or bad thing.

Good things	Bad things
Receive letter from Marmie Uncle and Aunt start being nice	Frightened by noise, people, leaving Seasick

- Fill in the events on the game board.
To play the game, you will need a dice and a playing piece for each player, made from thin card.

Photocopiable — Read & Respond — Coming to England

'The journey' game board

Receive letter from Marmie. Go forward 6.				
	Auntie and Uncle start being nice. Go forward 4.	Seasick. Go back 5.		
Bewildered and scared at the harbour. Go back 4.				

Coming to England

Photocopiable

Life in England

This is what Floella wrote about her first experiences of home in England:

> Was this it? Surely this couldn't be what we had travelled thousands of miles for… All I knew was this was not what I wanted my new home to be.

- Read from 'Land of Hope and Glory' to 'The Big Move'.
- List the differences between Floella's life in Trinidad and her life in England, using the topics given. Add any others that you find.

Look back at the first five chapters for the information on Trinidad and the chapters above for information on England.

	In Trinidad	In England
The home and garden		
The weather		
The countryside		
Playground games		
Religion		
Shopping		
Outings		

- On balance, which place do you think Floella preferred? Explain why you think so.
- She writes on page 80: "I felt like a fish out of water." What do you think she means?

Write your answers on the back of this sheet.

Photocopiable — Read & Respond — Coming to England

Double identity

● Read 'Double Identity'. How did Floella cope with her new life? She describes herself as having two identities – one at school and one at home. Decide which of the following belongs with which of Floella's two identities and link them to the correct illustration with a line. Use a different colour for each identity.

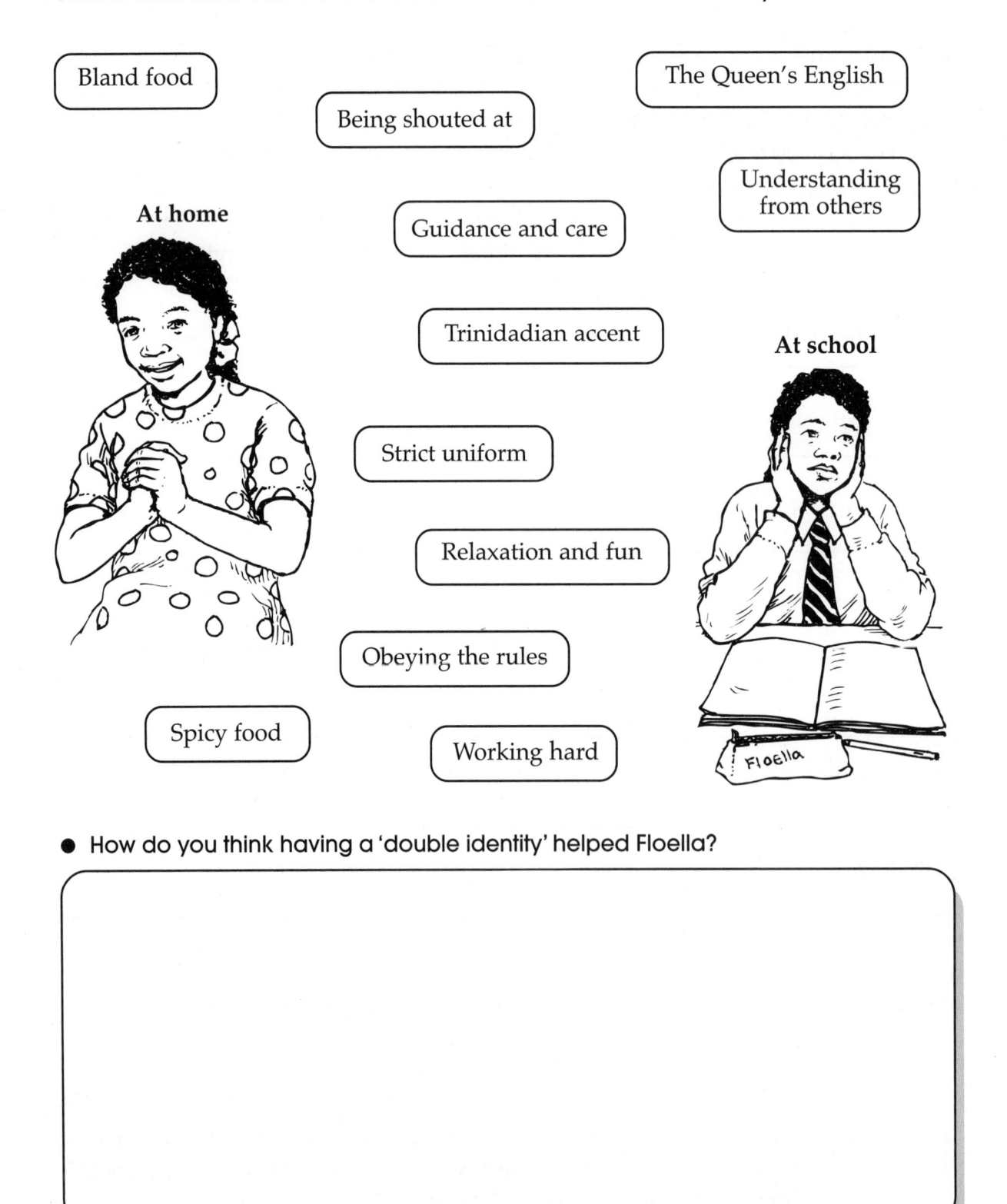

Bland food

Being shouted at

The Queen's English

Understanding from others

At home

Guidance and care

Trinidadian accent

At school

Strict uniform

Relaxation and fun

Obeying the rules

Spicy food

Working hard

● How do you think having a 'double identity' helped Floella?

Coming to England

Photocopiable

Success

● Read the last chapter, 'Breaking Down the Barriers'. Fill in the comments you think Floella's teachers would make on her end-of-year report.

Name: Floella Benjamin

Date: Class:

English

Mathematics

French

History

Geography

Music

Art

PE

Headmistress's comments:

Marmie

- Find and read the dedication. Why do you think Floella chose this dedication?
- Gather information from the book about Marmie. Use the headings to organize your findings.

These pages will help:
3; 8–12; 16; 25–6; 33; 42; 66–7; 82–3; 94–8; 100–1; 104; 107; 112; 116.

What things is Marmie good at?
Making beautiful clothes

Some things she says
Eat well to grow up big and strong

Things she believes
British education is the best in the world

Coming to England

Marmie (cont.)

Things she does for the family
Keeps the house clean and tidy

Adjectives that describe Marmie's personality…
Proud

…and appearance
Strong

How she adapts to England
Learns to drive

● Now you can be Marmie's biographer and write a character study of her. Include as many facts about her as you wish, but as her biographer you can also say what you think and feel about her.

The Queen's English

In 'Double Identity', Floella says she learned to speak one way at school and another way at home.

Who says this?

Who to?

What do you think she means?

> If you want to stay in my class and be understood by everyone you will learn to speak the Queen's English.

> My beloved Trinidadian accent, with its rich tones, was not lost; I just had to learn to use it at the appropriate time.

Who says this?

Who to?

Lots of people change the way they speak, depending on
- who they are speaking to
- where they are.
- How would you say the following?

Apologizing for something

to a friend

to your parents

to a teacher

Coming to England — Photocopiable

The Queen's English (cont.)

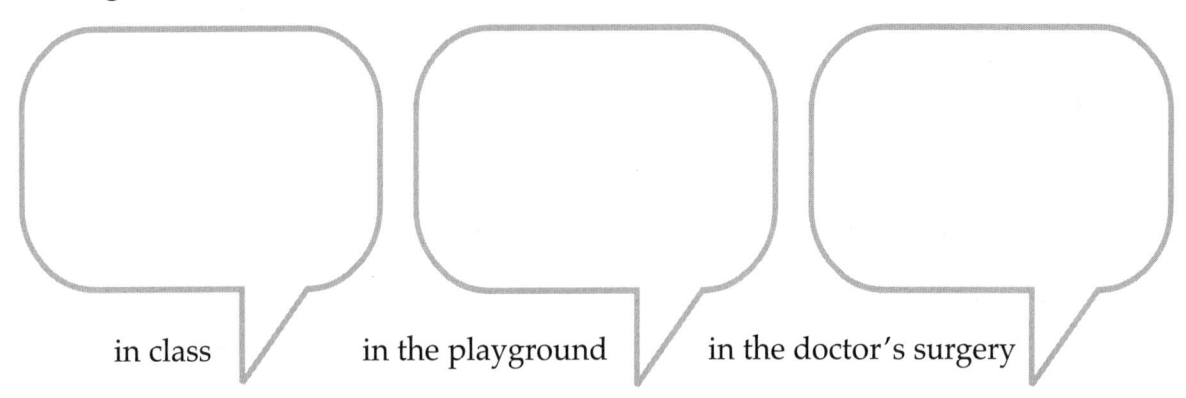

Feeling sick or ill

in class in the playground in the doctor's surgery

Greeting

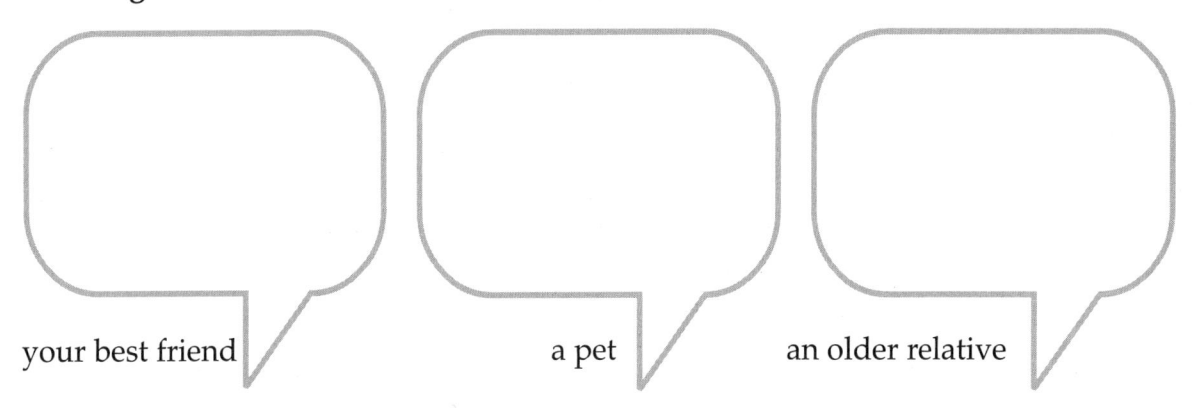

your best friend a pet an older relative

Asking how they are

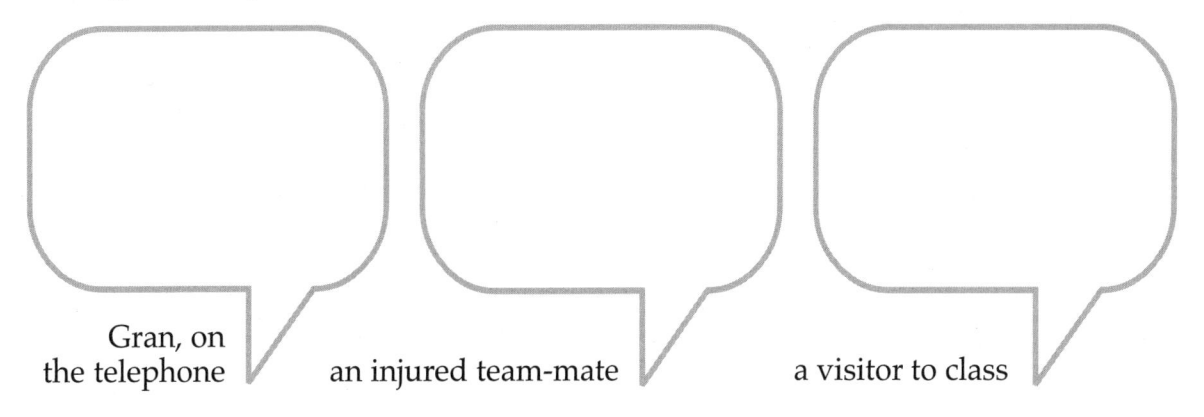

Gran, on the telephone an injured team-mate a visitor to class

How we say things is affected by the way we say them – how we pronounce the words. This is accent.
- Do you speak with an accent?
- Is your accent stronger at home or at school?
- Can you think why this might be?
- Can you speak in other accents?

Ellington's fight

In 'Life at Sea', Floella describes Ellington's fight on board the ship.
- Look back at pages 56–8, then draw four pictures to make a storyboard that retells the story of the fight. Add a caption for each sketch.

1	2
3	4

Later, the children tell the story to Cynthia and Junior:

> They loved hearing the story of Ellington nearly falling into the ocean, which got more and more exaggerated depending on who was telling the tale.

- Use your storyboard to retell the story aloud. Practise being Ellington. How would he change the story? Then practise being Sandra telling the story. What would she say? Present your different versions to a partner or to your group.

Coming to England — Photocopiable

Weather

I began to understand why the English always talked about the weather. There was so much of it.

● Look at 'Darkness & Light' and 'Survival'. Add to the barometer readings to show how the weather made Floella feel and behave.

Hot
Blue cloudless skies
Bright sunshine
Occasional cool sea breeze
Dark
Foggy
Blanket of snow
Strong clear light
Cold

Photocopiable

Coming to England

Names

The poet Jackie Kay said in an interview:

> I think I first became aware of racism when I went to school. Other kids at school would call me names or tell racist jokes or follow me, and I found all this upsetting and humiliating. But I made it my business to fight back.

She also wrote this poem:

Names

Today my best pal, *my number one*,
called me a *dirty darkie*,
when I wouldn't give her a sweetie.
I said, softly, "I would never believe
you of all people, Char Hardy,
would say that word to me.
Others, yes, the ones
that are stupid and ignorant,
and don't know better, but
not you, Char Hardy, not you.
I thought I could trust you.
I thought you were different.
But I must have been mistaken."

Char went a very strange colour.
Said a most peculiar, "Sorry,"
as if she was swallowing her voice.
Grabbed me, hugged me, begged me
to forgive her. She was crying.
I didn't mean it. I didn't mean it.
I felt the playground sink. *Sorry. Sorry.*
A see-saw rocked, crazy, all by itself.
An orange swing swung high on its own.
My voice was hard as a steel frame:
"Well then, what exactly did you mean?"

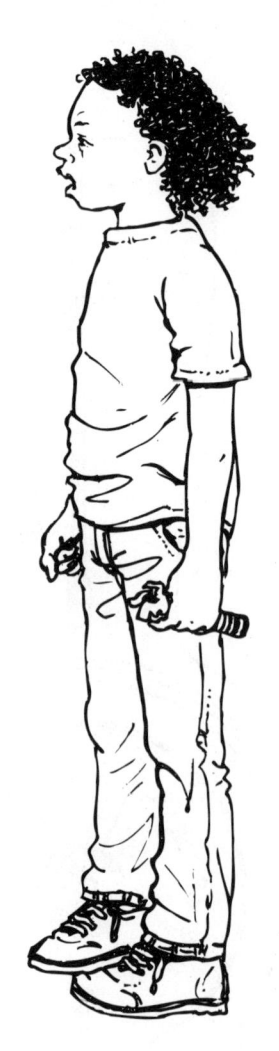

Coming to England

Photocopiable

Names (cont.)

● Do Jackie Kay's experiences remind you of anything in *Coming to England*? Think about:
- what people said and did
- how the writers react.

Look at pages: 81–2; 95; 100–1.

What did Floella's teachers think about black children?

What did some of the school children think about black children?

What did some of the neighbours think of black families?

How did the family 'fight back'?

Land of Hope and Glory

In 'Survival', Floella writes:

> I came to England feeling special, like a princess, but was made to feel like a scavenger, begging for a piece of what I thought was mine.

● Make notes on the ideas of England Floella was taught in Trinidad. Then make some on what she found when she arrived.

Look at pages:
18–20; 39–40; 71; 75; 81–3; 89–95; 99–101; 109; 112–14; 119–21.

Views of England – from Trinidad

"We were encouraged to feel proud that we were British." (page 20)
"We were taught the British Way… because it was considered to be the best education in the world." (page 19)
England is "as cold as an iceberg." (page 64)

Views of England – from England

Why was Floella so disappointed when she arrived in England?

Did her feelings change?

Coming to England

Photocopiable

Interviewing Floella Benjamin

You are going to interview Floella Benjamin for a television programme, but she can only spare you 10 minutes. You will need to have your best questions ready. What are you going to ask her?

● Think about things that viewers might like to know about her life and where she grew up. Avoid 'closed' questions that can be answered with just "Yes" or "No" – you need to draw out as much interesting material as possible in the time you have. Write your chosen questions below.

R&R news

Date: Programme:

Interviewee: Interviewer:

1.

2.

3.

4.

5.

● Practise your interview technique by asking a partner to 'be' Floella and to answer your questions in role.

EVALUATION

Afterword

- Re-read the 'Afterword' at the end of the book.

What does Floella say are her reasons for writing *Coming to England*?

Do you think she has succeeded? What effect has her book had on you?

Before I read Coming to England, I thought autobiography was

From reading Coming to England, I have learned that autobiography is

Coming to England

READ & RESPOND

Photocopiable

USING THIS BOOK

Coming to England is a simply told book accessible to a wide range of readers, but it deals with serious and sensitive issues: racism, language, identity, and moral, personal and family values. It is an autobiography that tells about the real-life story of the writer so children need to realize that it is non-fiction.

Reading and discussing the book could be painful and difficult for some children as our responses to autobiographies raise issues about our own lives and attitudes.

Although the book deals with the racism that Floella Benjamin and her family were victims of when they came to England, the story also brings out the happiness of living in a close-knit, loving and supportive family. It is about believing in yourself and being determined to succeed whatever the odds.

The book offers rich opportunities for reading and writing development. It introduces children to a very accessible genre – autobiography. Although autobiography is non-fiction, it is narrative in form. *Coming to England* is simply written and provides a good model for children's own writing. Finding something to write about is the first hurdle for many children. Focusing on events that they have experienced, rather than drawing exclusively on their imaginations, allows them to concentrate on their writing skills. Having firsthand experience of an event helps children to recreate it and bring it alive for the reader through vivid use of language. Reading the autobiographical accounts of other people triggers memories and provides interesting discussions that encourage writing.

MANAGING THE READING OF *COMING TO ENGLAND*

The introductory and **Ways in** activities are designed to be carried out before the book is read. They are all intended to introduce the children to autobiography as a form of writing. The starting point is their own lives and the people, places and events that they remember. This preparatory work could be developed in guided writing and independent writing sessions to support the children's own writing. The autobiography checklists introduce the children to the main linguistic features of the genre and then ask them to find specific examples from this book. The final **Ways in** activity uses some of the chapter titles for the children to predict what is going to happen.

Thus prepared for the kind of book they are going to be reading, the children should read *Coming to England* in six sections; each supported by a **Making sense** activity designed to focus on the key elements in that section. The activities provide opportunities for the children to reflect on and discuss what they have read to enrich their understanding and inform their reading.

The **Developing ideas** and **Evaluation** activities are intended to be worked on after the initial reading. They are designed to encourage the children to re-read, to read some pages more closely and to skim and scan others. They offer opportunities for children to develop a considered and personal response to their reading by responding to it through a variety of activities.

CLASSROOM MANAGEMENT AND SUPPORT

Coming to England can be read by individuals, a group or the whole class. Any reading to the whole class or in guided reading needs to be interspersed with discussion of what has been previously read. Many of the activities are suitable for whole-class, small-group, pair or individual work (see the teaching points in **Teachers' notes** on pages 29–32). Certain activities are particularly suitable for:

- whole class – all of the **Ways in** activities
- groups – 'Life in Trinidad' (pages 8–9) and 'The journey' (pages 11–12); 'The Queen's English' (pages 18–19) and 'Land of Hope and Glory' (page 24); 'Interviewing Floella Benjamin' (page 25)
- pairs – 'The family breaks up' (page 10) and 'Life in England' (page 13); 'The Queen's English' (pages 18–19), 'Ellington's fight' (page 20) and 'Weather' (page 21).

Some of the activities require children to re-read a particular part of the book. These are marked with the icon 📖. It is advisable to invest in at least six copies of the book so that groups and pairs can work independently. If the whole class is working on the book, plan the lesson so that some children are doing activities that require copies of the book while others are working on activities that can be done without direct access to the text.

Make sure you give the children ample opportunity to share and discuss their work.

Coming to England

HELP!

DIFFERENTIATION
There is a wide range of activities in this book, most of which provide for differentiation by response and outcome rather than task. They are aimed at children in Years 5 and 6 (Primary 6 and 7). Their content relates to the teaching objectives of the National Literacy Strategy. You will need to plan to support children who may find some of the material difficult.

Each activity has a learning core which is given as its 'Aim' in the teachers' notes. Children will achieve these aims to varying degrees. The activities are not intended to be slavishly followed and not all of them need to be done by all the children, particularly in the **Developing ideas** section. Children can work concurrently on different activities then share findings, allowing all the children access to the full range of tasks and involving them in presentation work. The extension activities in the **Teachers' notes** offer challenges to more able readers and writers.

TIME-SCALE
This will depend on the approach adopted and whether or not the book is being used as a whole-class text. *Read & Respond* books are intended to encourage reflection and in-depth study in order to develop reading skills.

MATCHING THE BOOK TO YOUR CLASS
Coming to England is a book which appeals to both boys and girls. It works well with children at the top of Key Stage 2 as it requires a fairly mature response to the serious issues that it raises. However, apart from the references to exotic food, the vocabulary level of the narrative is not high. It is also not a particularly long book and its structure is straightforward. Although it is a non-fiction text, it is easily accessible to children because of its narrative form.

TEACHING POTENTIAL OF *COMING TO ENGLAND*
The skills grid on the inside back cover provides an overview of the areas of the English curriculum covered by this book. *Coming to England* can be especially useful in introducing children to non-fiction through an accessible genre and provides a wonderful opportunity to develop children's writing. It can also be used to lead on to an exploration of biography.

Cross-curricular links
Coming to England offers learning opportunities in:
- history – the British Empire and Commonwealth
- geography – the contrast between the Caribbean and England
- PSHE and citizenship – this is the richest area for extension as *Coming to England* covers a wide range of important issues, such as racism, language and culture, identity, values, family life.

GLOSSARY
The children will need to know the following terms:
- non-fiction
- writing in the first person
- skim and scan
- character study.

RECOMMENDED PREVIOUS TEACHING
The children should be familiar with the idea that there are different kinds of writing and that they have different characteristics and purposes.

RESOURCES
The children may find it helpful to have access to a good dictionary, atlas and reference books where they can research Trinidad and its food, weather and lifestyle. History books and maps of the British Empire would also be useful.

FURTHER READING
Other autobiographies and biographies
The Diary of a Young Girl by Anne Frank (Puffin Books)
Zlata's Diary by Zlata Filipovic (Heinemann Education)
Telling Tales – a series of biographies on children's authors (Egmont Children's Books)
Other books with a similar inspirational message
Amazing Grace and *Grace and Family* by Mary Hoffman and Caroline Binch (Frances Lincoln)

Coming to England

TEACHERS' NOTES

COMING TO ENGLAND BY FLOELLA BENJAMIN (PAGE 3)
Aim: to help the children understand that the book has been written by the author about her own life, that it is real.
Teaching points: linking with prior knowledge, see if the children have read any other autobiographies or biographies? What is the difference? Do they know who Floella Benjamin is apart from the author of this book?

THIS IS YOUR LIFE (PAGE 4)
Aim: to begin to explore the genre by starting with reflections about the children's lives and what they know, remember and have been told about them; to encourage them to use this information to write their autobiographies; to think about the genre and its form.
Teaching points: some knowledge of the children's private lives is essential here as it could be a very sensitive area for some children.
Extension: any of the things that the children come up with while making their notes could be explored further, for example in a display of baby photographs or memorabilia. Children could be asked to write fragments of their autobiography that they could work on as they read *Coming to England*, using the book both as a model and a stimulus.

WHAT IS AUTOBIOGRAPHY? (PAGE 5)
Aim: to introduce children to the general characteristics and linguistic features of the genre.
Teaching points: this page could be enlarged and used as a shared text.
Extension: the children could go through the list a second time with a different-coloured pen to highlight points that could also apply to fiction. This could lead to a discussion about the differences between fiction and non-fiction, autobiography and biography.

IS IT AUTOBIOGRAPHY? (PAGE 6)
Aim: to transfer the children's knowledge about genre to this particular text by finding examples of autobiography characteristics that are evident in the text.
Teaching points: although the children will not have started reading the book yet, there are examples in the text listed to draw out comparisons with other autobiographies and fiction texts that they have read.
Extension: as the children read through the book, continue to demonstrate how the book's structure and style fit the genre.

CHAPTER TITLES (PAGE 7)
Aims: to predict what might happen in the book using some of the chapter headings; to reinforce understanding of the kind of book it is and that the chapters will be based on fact.
Teaching points: use the prediction exercise to reiterate the characteristics of the genre so that the children appreciate that the book is based on fact.
Extension: the children could come back to their predictions after they have read the book and see how closely they matched up with actual events.

LIFE IN TRINIDAD (PAGES 8–9)
Aims: to explore the setting of the first part of the book and to understand and appreciate what the main character's life was like before she moved to England; to skim and scan and extract information; to make notes.
Teaching points: this is an activity that requires reading a substantial chunk of the text first. It will take time, but it is necessary to establish Floella's lifestyle before the move so that the children can appreciate the contrast.
Extension: the children could use the information to give presentations or mount displays on the topics; they could research Trinidad using reference books, CD-ROMs and websites.

HELP!

THE FAMILY BREAKS UP (PAGE 10)
Aims: to explore the development of the story by focusing on a pivotal chapter in the structure of the book; to contrast circumstances; to re-present information in another form.
Teaching points: this is an activity that could be done with the whole class or in pairs. The children need to understand that it is a pivotal chapter.
Extension: the children could write diary entries in role as the other children in the family, letters written to Marmie before they were censored or letters from the parents to the children.

THE JOURNEY (PAGES 11–12)
Aims: to summarize the story so far; to make judgements about events – whether they were good or bad.
Teaching points: this could be done as a whole-class activity, and you may want to enlarge the board. The children will need support in deciding on the main events and some may need help in translating events into moves on the board, for example deciding how many spaces forward or back a particular event should take them.

Suggested good events that would move the players forward: receive letter from Marmie about coming to England; Auntie and Uncle start being nice to the children; ship leaves harbour; see flying fish; enjoying life on board; see Marmie; new cardigan; Marmie cooks a meal. Bad things that would move the players back: frightened by noise and saying goodbye; seasick; fighting on boat; horrible food; frightened on underground; being stared at; upset and disappointed by new home.

As well as the events causing moves backwards or forwards they could also result in missing a go or having another go.

Writing the instructions for the game could be an extension exercise but some basic rules for playing the game will need to be decided, such as: Do the players need to throw a six to start? Do they need the exact number of moves to land on 'Home' and finish the game? Do players get an extra turn if they throw a six? These decisions could be made in small groups or as a class.
Extension: help the children to write the instructions on how to play the game. This could involve looking at other game instructions and considering the language and style of instruction texts. The instructions could be word-processed and kept with the board or made into a display.

LIFE IN ENGLAND (PAGE 13)
Aim: to focus on the effect of the move on the main character and the contrast between the life she left behind and her new life.
Teaching points: children might need support in understanding how and why the reality of life in England did not match up to expectations. They can refer back to the work that they did on the opening chapters.

Possible answers to page 12

Coming to England

READ & RESPOND

DOUBLE IDENTITY (PAGE 14)
Aim: to understand the main character and the complicated life she leads.
Teaching points: the concept of a double identity may be very familiar to some children, others may have difficulty in understanding it. It is crucial that the children appreciate how Floella coped and retained her confidence and courage.
Extension: children could be asked to write in role as Floella, at home and at school, to demonstrate the two identities. They could detail two days in her life, comparing a school day with a day spent with her family.

SUCCESS (PAGE 15)
Aims: to understand how others see the main character; to represent information given in the book to demonstrate close reading and comprehension.
Teaching points: gathering the information could be done as a whole-class activity. Children may need guidance on the kind of comments wanted and language to be used. This could be modelled in a whole-class session or in guided writing.
Extension: children could write the parents' response to the report or perform a role-play of a parents' evening when the report is discussed by teachers and parents.

MARMIE (PAGES 16–17)
Aims: to write a character study of a key character; to write in the first person; to examine biography as a genre and link it to autobiography.
Teaching points: some children may need support for this activity. They need to appreciate that it works in stages and that they will not be able to begin writing the character study until they have gathered, and organized, their relevant information.
Extension: the information could be used to 'hot-seat' Marmie (played by you or one of the children) for her to answer questions from the class in role.

THE QUEEN'S ENGLISH (PAGES 18–19)
Aim: to develop language awareness through considering the importance of context, audience and accent.
Teaching points: depending on the linguistic diversity in the class, this may need careful handling as accent in particular can be felt as a social class issue. Children might need help in understanding that standard English can be spoken with an accent. Point out that, although Floella emphasizes the importance of her accent, she writes *Coming to England* in standard English and does not attempt to write with an accent. This could lead on to a discussion about the difference between spoken and written English and the difficulties of understanding text written with an accent.
Extension: this activity could lead to more work on standard English, slang, accent and dialect. Children could produce mini-dictionaries of slang or dialect, read writing written in an accent or dialect and translate it into Standard English or vice versa.

ELLINGTON'S FIGHT (PAGE 20)
Aims: to summarize the main points of the event and to develop oral skills; to explore using different narrators to tell different versions of the event.
Teaching points: the quality of the pictures should not be an issue; it is the content and the caption that is important.
Extension: ask the children to write the event as a conversation or playscript.

WEATHER (PAGE 21)
Aims: to explore a theme in the book; to re-present information in a different format.
Teaching points: children might need help in understanding that the weather is more than just the difference between it being hot or cold, or wet or dry, and that the weather can influence feelings and behaviour.

HELP!

NAMES (PAGES 22-3)
Aim: to explore one of the main themes of the book and to compare and contrast the experience of one writer with that of another.
Teaching points: this is a very sensitive issue that needs careful handling, but it is such an important subject in the book that it should not be avoided.
Extension: children could write about their own experiences of being bullied. The poem could be worked on in pairs to be presented as a performance reading – the children would have to examine it closely to fully grasp the meaning and to be able to use the right emphasis and intonation.

LAND OF HOPE AND GLORY (PAGE 24)
Aim: to continue the exploration of the central character and her experiences to understand her feelings.
Teaching points: the children might need to be helped to understand that because Trinidad had been a British colony the people who lived there considered themselves British. Floella did not expect to be treated like an outsider when she came to England.

INTERVIEWING FLOELLA BENJAMIN (PAGE 25)
Aims: to aid comprehension and personal response; to consolidate understanding about the book.
Teaching points: the children should be encouraged to think carefully about the questions that they would ask to demonstrate the depth of their understanding of the book. Some children might need help in choosing appropriate questions. The children need to be able to match the experiences in the book to Floella Benjamin's later life and see how the events in the book contributed to her later success and lifestyle. The time limit should help them to focus their questions. Encourage them also to think about the typical phrasing and language of interview questions. Referring to television interviews and chat shows that the children have seen might be useful.
Extension: children could write an article about Floella Benjamin for a magazine, or a feature about the interview for the *Radio Times*.

AFTERWORD (PAGE 26)
Aim: to deepen understanding about the book and the genre.
Teaching points: this is an opportunity for children to reflect on their reading of *Coming to England*. They should be encouraged to talk about their response to the book and discuss what they have learned about autobiography in general. Tell them to think carefully before writing or discussing their answers. They could be directed to look at their work on genre from the first sessions.

Coming to England